Gallery Books
Editor: Peter Fallon

THE FLOWER MASTER
AND OTHER POEMS

Medbh McGuckian

'THE FLOWER MASTER
MASTER
AND OTHER POEMS '

Gallery Books

The Flower Master and Other Poems
is first published
simultaneously in paperback
and in a clothbound edition
on 11 November 1993.

The Gallery Press
Loughcrew
Oldcastle
County Meath
Ireland

ISBN 1 85235 124 1 (*paperback*)
     1 85235 125 X (*clothbound*)

The Gallery Press receives financial assistance from An Chomhairle
Ealaíon / The Arts Council, Ireland, and acknowledges also the assis-
tance of the Arts Council of Northern Ireland in the publication of this
book.

Contents

for my mother
without my father

Smoke

They set the whins on fire along the road.
I wonder what controls it, can the wind hold
That snake of orange motion to the hills,
Away from the houses?

They seem so sure what they can do.
I am unable even
To contain myself, I run
Till the fawn smoke settles on the earth.

Faith

My grandmother led us to believe in snow
As an old man in the sky shaking
Feathers down from his mattress over the world.

Her bed in the morning was covered with tiny scales,
Sloughed off in the night from peeling skin;
They floated in a cloud

Of silver husks to the floor, or spun
In the open window like starry litter,
Blowing along the road.

I burned them in a heap, a dream of coins
More than Thérèse's promised shower of roses,
Or Virgil's souls, many as Autumn leaves.

Spring

It was cold in the bed with my sister,
The street lamps swollen as crocuses.
She was sleeping soundly when I rose
To stare at the February moon.

The curtains slit at my hand,
My breathing marbled the pane:
There was my face in the window,
Frosted, so hard to see through.

The 'Singer'

In the evenings I used to study
At my mother's old sewing-machine,
Pressing my feet occasionally
Up and down on the treadle
As though I were going somewhere
I had never been.

Every year at exams, the pressure mounted —
The summer light bent across my pages
Like a squinting eye. The children's shouts
Echoed the weather of the street,
A car was thunder,
The ticking of a clock was heavy rain . . . .

In the dark I drew the curtains
On young couples stopping in the entry,
Heading home. There were nights
I sent the disconnected wheel
Spinning madly round and round
Till the empty bobbin rattled in its case.

Eavesdropper

That year it was something to do with your hands:
To play about with rings, to harness rhythm
In staging bleach or henna on the hair,
Or shackling, unshackling the breasts.

I remembered as a child the red kite
Lost forever over our heads, the white ball
A pin-prick on the tide, and studied
The leaf-patterned linoleum, the elaborate

Stitches on my pleated bodice.
It was like a bee's sting or a bullet
Left in me, this mark, this sticking pins in dolls,
Listening for the red and white

Particles of time to trickle slow, like a wet nurse
Feeding nonchalantly someone else's child.
I wanted curtainings, and cushionings;
The grass is an eavesdropper's bed.

Mr McGregor's Garden

Some women save their sanity with needles.
I complicate my life with studies
Of my favourite rabbit's head, his vulgar volatility,
Or a little ladylike sketching
Of my resident toad in his flannel box;
Or search for handsome fungi for my tropical
Herbárium, growing dry-rot in the garden,
And wishing that the climate were kinder,
Turning over the spiky purple heads among the moss
With my cheese-knife to view the slimy veil.

Unlike the cupboard-love of sleepers in the siding,
My hedgehog's sleep is under his control
And not the weather's; he can rouse himself
At half-an-hour's notice in the frost, or leave at will
On a wet day in August, by the hearth.
He goes by breathing slowly, after a large meal,
A lively evening, very cross if interrupted,
And returns with a hundred respirations
To the minute, weak and nervous when he wakens,
Busy with his laundry.

On sleepless nights while learning
Shakespeare off by heart,
I feel that Bunny's at my bedside
In a white cotton nightcap,
Tickling me with his whiskers.

Chopping

Close your eyes
Unwinding the bitter onion —
Its layers of uncertainty are limited,
Under brown paper its sealed heart sings
To the tune of a hundred lemons.

Today I am feeling up to it:
I bend my throat aside —
There is no pain, only the soft entrances
Again, again, the vegetable's
Finely numbered bones.

The Long Engagement

1

In my all-weather loneliness I am like a sparrow
Picking leftovers of rice in a mortar,
A dark cicada clinging to a branch,
The empty space created by your kiss;

Occasionally, as Sunday silver, sit
In a quiet, eastward-facing room,
And make a thread from the fibres of the five signs
Leading to the eight valleys, my lush palace gate.

2

I lie down thirsty from the thunderstorm,
Visualizing first this book, the objects on the tray,
Then you asleep, my loosening
Towards your pointed ceiling,

Through half-open lids your hand,
Repeat your name, and count the laddered
Steps to your house, till I fall
Backwards through the salted folds, the spring of your door.

3

You overflow, sleeping on your back:
My lap is bent upon itself, my bulbs
Are fleeced, my wishbone wings are tied.

Perhaps my worry beads need sanding —
All they ask is to be lifted from their winding
Cold, the subsidence of their avenues.

Lychees

You wonder at that Georgian terrace
Miles out of town where the motorway begins.
My great-grandfather was a coachman
And knew how far away he was in the dark
By mysteries of the Rosary. My grandmother said
You could tell a good husband
By the thumbed leaves of his prayer-book.

A dead loss, my mother counts you,
Setting my teeth on edge at all hours,
Getting me to break the lychee's skin.
She underestimates the taste of sacrifice,
The irrelevance of distances,
Cat's-eyes, the cleanness of hands.

Slips

The studied poverty of a moon roof,
The earthenware of dairies cooled by apple trees,
The apple tree that makes the whitest wash . . .

But I forget names, remembering them wrongly
Where they touch upon another name,
A town in France like a woman's Christian name.

My childhood is preserved as a nation's history,
My favourite fairytales the shells
Leased by the hermit crab.

I see my grandmother's death as a piece of ice,
My mother's slimness restored to her,
My own key slotted in your door —

Tricks you might guess from this unfastened button,
A pen mislaid, a word misread,
My hair coming down in the middle of a conversation.

Aunts

My aunts jived their way
Through the '50s to my teens.
They lay till noon and called me up
To listen for their lovers at the gate,
And paid me for the colour of their eyes —
'Grey,' I said, or 'Brown,' when they wanted
Blue or hazel, in their giggling,
Sleeping-together dreams.

I watched them shading in their lips
From sugar pink to coral, from mulberry to rose,
And their wet skirts hungry for
The brilliance of their swing,
As they dried by the strange
Elastic girdles, paper petticoats.

Once out of the blue
I caught them dancing on the bed,
With their undergrowth of hazel,
And their make-up sweated through.

My Mother

My mother's smell is sweet or sour and moist
Like the soft red cover of the apple.
She sits among her boxes, lace and tins,
And notices the smallest of all breezes,
As if she were a tree upon the mountain
Growing away with no problem at all.

Her swan's head quivers like a light-bulb:
Does she breed in perfect peace, a light sleep,
Or smothered like a clock whose alarm
Is unendurable, whose featureless
Straight face is never wrong?
No one knows what goes on inside a clock.

The Hollywood Bed

We narrow into the house, the room, the bed,
Where sleep begins its shunting. You adopt
Your mask, your intellectual cradling of the head,
Neat as notepaper in your creaseless
Envelope of clothes, while I lie crosswise,
Imperial as a favoured only child,
Calmed by sagas of how we lay like spoons
In a drawer, till you blew open
My tightened bud, my fully-buttoned housecoat,
Like some Columbus mastering
The saw-toothed waves, the rows of letter *m*s.

Now the headboard is disturbed
By your uncomfortable skew, your hands
Like stubborn adverbs visiting your face,
Or your shoulder, in your piquancy of dreams,
The outline that, if you were gone,
Would find me in your place.

The Sofa

Do not be angry if I tell you
Your letter stayed unopened on my table
For several days. If you were friend enough
To believe me, I was about to start writing
At any moment; my mind was savagely made up,
Like a serious sofa moved
Under a north window. My heart, alas,

Is not the calmest of places.
Still it is not my heart that needs replacing:
And my books seem real enough to me,
My disasters, my surrenders, all my loss . . . .
Since I was child enough to forget
That you loathe poetry, you ask for some —
About nature, greenery, insects, and, of course,

The sun — surely that would be to open
An already open window? To celebrate
The impudence of flowers? If I could
Interest you instead in his large, gentle stares,
How his soft shirt is the inside of pleasure
To me, why I must wear white for him,
Imagine he no longer trembles

When I approach, no longer buys me
Flowers for my name day . . . . But I spread
On like a house, I begin to scatter
To a tiny to-and-fro at odds
With the wear on my threshold. Somewhere
A curtain rising wonders where I am,
My books sleep, pretending to forget me.

To My Grandmother

I would revive you with a swallow's nest:
For as long a time as I could hold my breath
I would feel your pulse like tangled weeds
Separate into pearls. The heart should rule
The summer, ringing like a sickle over
The need to make life hard. I would
Sedate your eyes with rippleseed, those
Hollow points that close as if
Your eyelids had been severed
To deny you sleep, imagine you a dawn.
I would push a chrysanthemum stone
Into your sleeve without your noticing
Its reaching far, its going, its returning.
When the end of summer comes, it is
A season by itself; when your tongue
Curls back like a sparrow's buried head,
I would fill your mouth with rice and mussels.

Tulips

Touching the tulips was a shyness
I had had for a long time — such
Defensive mechanisms to frustrate the rain
That shakes into the sherry-glass
Of the daffodil, though scarcely
Love's young dream; such present-mindedness
To double-lock in tiers as whistle-tight,
Or catch up on sleep with cantilevered
Palms cupping elbows.

It's their independence
Tempts them to this grocery of soul.

Except, like all governesses, easily
Carried away, they sun themselves
Exaltedly to ballets of revenge,
A kind of twinness, an olympic
Mode of earning: their absent faces
Lifted many times to the artistry of light —
Its lovelessness a deeper sort
Of illness than the womanliness
Of tulips with their bee-dark hearts.

The Seed-Picture

This is my portrait of Joanna — since the split
The children come to me like a dumb-waiter,
And I wonder where to put them, beautiful seeds
With no immediate application . . . the clairvoyance
Of seed-work has opened up
New spectrums of activity, beyond a second home.
The seeds dictate their own vocabulary,
Their dusty colours capture
More than we can plan,
The mould on walls, or jumbled garages,
Dead flower heads where insects shack . . . .
I only guide them not by guesswork
In their necessary numbers,
And attach them by the spine to a perfect bedding,
Woody orange pips, and tear-drop apple,
The banana of the caraway, wrinkled peppercorns,
The pocked peach, or waterlily honesty,
The seamed cherry stone so hard to break.

Was it such self-indulgence to enclose her
In the border of a grandmother's sampler,
Bonding all the seeds in one continuous skin,
The sky resolved to a cloud the length of a man?
To use tan linseed for the trees, spiky
Sunflower for leaves, bright lentils
For the window, patna stars
For the floral blouse? Her hair
Is made of hook-shaped marigold, gold
Of pleasure for her lips, like raspberry grain.

The eyelids oatmeal, the irises
Of Dutch blue maw, black rape
For the pupils, millet
For the vicious beige circles underneath.
The single pearl barley
That sleeps around her dullness
Till it catches light, makes women
Feel their age, and sigh for liberation.

The Sun-Trap

Our lean-to greenhouse lends
Quite a sun-trap in the mornings,
Where I page you from this sickly Irish weather.
And the hygroscope says 'orchid',
Though in winter it stays blue,
Unless placed between the window and the storm-sash.

I am touched by even the strange gesture
Of rain stopping, your penetration
Of my mask of 'bon viveur', my crested notepaper,
My lined envelopes. From your last letter
I construed at least the word
For kisses, if not quite a kindred spirit.

But my night has been chequered
By toothache, and your reference
To the magically fertile German girl
Who sleeps in the bunk above you
At the workcamp. She seems
To me quite flirtatious

Though you say she's the sort of girl
You'd rather have as a daughter —
Which reminds me of my cousin once-removed,
And the near-tragedy
Of our long pony-trekking weekend . . . .
You find it odd I should resurrect him

Just when I seemed
To be losing
My wholesome curiosity in corpses?
Miles from anywhere, if you could learn
From other people's letters to me,
We might talk as human beings are supposed to.

Gladiolus

This border plant whose stately flowers clone
Their saturated reds on a single stem
Will not exhaust the ground like the bushy dahlia:
Its only aim the art
Of making oneself loved,
It grows in transit with the satiny moons
Of honesty, stepping free even of its own
Foliage, evergreen or evergrey, its collared
Leaves overlying, and its grains ripped
Benignly like so many kernels, like a thousand
Cards shuffled in a roguish draught, to catch
The daughter-cells, the reason for these yellow scars.

The Orchid House

1

A flower's fragrance is a woman's virtue;
So I tell them underground in pairs,
Or in their fleshy white sleeves, how
Desirable their shapes, how one
Was lost for sixty years, with all
Its arching spikes, its honeyed tessellations,
And how in bloom they will resemble
Moths, the gloss of mirrors, Christmas
Stars, their helmets blushing
Red-brown when they marry.

2

In my alpine house, the slavery I pay
My wilful gentians, exploring all their pleats
And tucks as though they had something precious
Deep inside, that beard of camel-hair
In the throat. I watch them
Ease their heads so slowly
Through their thumbhole necklines, till they sit
Like tailors in their earth shoes,
Their watery husbands' knots. No insects
Visit them, nor do their ovaries swell,
Yet every night in Tibet their seeds
Are membraned by the snow, their roots
Are bathed by the passage of melt-water;
They tease like sullen spinsters
The dewfall of summer limes.

3

The disdain of green summer cloud
On our glasshouses has bred out
The tomato's coat of hair;

And flowers yield themselves less foolishly
Than deer that fan their cologne
With the affluence of flattened tears:

They must be harvested at dawn, before
Their permafrost has sunk beyond
A skater's melted world,

Rude as hyacinths encircling
A private room at night,
To this tall icicle, my geranium oil,

The spills of my patchoulied shawl.

4

The begonia's soil is rich and wet.
I tuck it in around her
As I would pat my hair,
Straightening her tubered root.

We keep our sources secret — she
Swells with lymph and electricity,
Her fibres transparently taped up, and I
Sprout willowy as any sweet begonia.

Your House

Our childless house has perfect teeth.
The running water of its lovemaking
Is pickled in silence, in a wicker-covered
Bottle, its fluorescence steadying itself
Into the barely breatheable importance
Even your servants' quarters nudge away,
Where you afford your matted walk-through
Rooms, with their creamy hems, their windows
Succouring the heart. The way they swing
Like the sickled gladiolus, swell your house ·
As Ireland's tiny mountains load her breast
Like a necklace! How they take the rain
In their eyes, and make all possible use
Of moonlight, as a sea-meadow
Becomes a bath of meadow-sweet
Under the goats' milk stars, till you might
Ring your bells, knowing someone would come.

Gateposts

A man will keep a horse for prestige,
But a woman ripens best underground.
He settles where the wind
Brings his whirling hat to rest,
And the wind decides which door is to be used.

Under the hip-roofed thatch,
The bed-wing is warmed by the chimney breast;
On either side the keeping-holes
For his belongings, hers.

He says it's unlucky to widen the house
And leaves the gateposts holding up the fairies.
He lays his lazy-beds and burns the river,
He builds turf-castles,
And sprigs the corn with apple-mint.

She spreads heather on the floor
And sifts the oatmeal ark for thin-bread farls:
All through the blue month, July,
She tosses stones in basins to the sun,
And watches for the trout in the holy well.

The Soil-Map

I am not a woman's man, but I can tell,
By the swinging of your two-leaf door,
You are never without one man in the shadow
Of another; and because the mind
Of a woman between two men is lighter
Than a spark, the petalled steps to your porch
Feel frigid with a lost warmth. I will not
Take you in hardness, for all the dark cage
Of my dreaming over your splendid fenestration,
Your moulded sills, your slender purlins,

The secret woe of your gutters. I will do it
Without niggardliness, like food with one
Generous; a moment as auspicious
And dangerous as the christening of a ship,
My going in to find the settlement
Of every floor, the hump of water
Following the moon, and her discolouring,
The saddling derangement of a roof
That might collapse its steepness
Under the sudden strain of clearing its name.

For anyone with patience can divine
How your plasterwork has lost key, the rendering
About to come away. So like a rainbird,
Challenged by a charm of goldfinch,
I appeal to the god who fashions edges
Whether such turning-points exist
As these saltings we believe we move
Away from, as if by simply shaking
A cloak we could disbud ourselves,
Dry out, and cease to live there?

I have found the places on the soil-map,
Proving it possible once more to call
Houses by their names, Annsgift or Mavisbank,
Mount Juliet or Bettysgrove: they should not
Lie with the gloom of disputes to interrupt them
Every other year, like some disease
Of language making humorous the friendship
Of the thighs. I drink to you as Hymenstown,
(My touch of fantasy) or First Fruits,
Impatient for my power as a bride.

The Swing

It's been quite a year for strange weather.
From speedy March to slow September,
The drought left firemen sleepless, Ireland
So like Italy Italians came to film it.
Each evening the Egyptian goddess
Swallowed the sun, her innocent
Collective pleasure, never minding his violent temper,
His copious emissions, how he sprinkled
The lawn of space till it became
A deadly freckled junkyard.

Looking at what is most important
Leaves me blind: without leaving my room
I might escape from waves in a Roman cage-cup
Made from a single piece of glass, and sail
My wafer yacht on the solar wind, my watered
Body, my earthy liquid centre, protected
By a crown. Wish me a mission
Trouble free; if I lose contact,
To die smiling of exhaustion, the invisible
Child upon a swing so I can almost touch his hands.

The Sunbench

Behind my party wall what bolts of silk
Prepare their images, relax from them
Like petals lolling in a knot garden
Voluptuous with rapid growth! These seed leaves
I have summered and these true leaves wintered
Through the spartan frost, supported by sweet
Chestnut, riven oak, till lime unlocks
Their mongrel tenderness, the shattering excretion
    of the rose . . . .

This is not the hardness of a single night,
A rib that I could clearly do without. It is
The room where you have eaten daily,
Shaking free like a hosting tree, the garden
Shaking off the night's weak appetite,
The sunbench brown and draining into fallow.

Champagne

1

It is not in our interest to be too attractive:
The frequent death of distant suns
That prey upon these sexless nights
Leaves me incapable of dream as birds.

An unobtrusive glance will trace
The far-off mocking star, the character
Shone by a flower on your neck, the shallow
Seconds between obligation and dawn.

2

The soulless matchmaking of lunar moths,
Uncanny, delicate or helpful, dove-coloured
Bosoms in the night: their fictions hurt us
Gently, like the nudity of rose-beige tea-gowns . . . .

The mayflies' opera is their only moon, only
Those that fall on water reproduce, content
With scattering in fog or storm, such ivory
As elephants hold lofty, like champagne.

The Flower Master

Like foxgloves in the school of the grass moon
We come to terms with shade, with the principle
Of enfolding space. Our scissors in brocade,
We learn the coolness of straight edges, how
To stroke gently the necks of daffodils
And make them throw their heads back to the sun.

We slip the thready stems of violets, delay
The loveliness of the hibiscus dawn with quiet ovals,
Spirals of feverfew like water splashing,
The papery legacies of bluebells. We do
Sea-fans with sea-lavender, moon-arrangements
Roughly for the festival of moon-viewing.

This black container calls for sloes, sweet
Sultan, dainty nipplewort, in honour
Of a special guest, who summoned to the
Tea ceremony, must stoop to our low doorway,
Our fontanelle, the trout's dimpled feet.

Fossils

This is in fact our only record of them,
As if they had found a breathing, a flotation chamber
Here in the mud, uncrushed as other
Fashionable experiments, these maturing
Soft-bodied males, no oxygen
Fuelling the cells of their decay.

Encountering no change, they see
No cause for change, as mantled
As the eggs in the paper cradle shell
The octopus secretes from his arm —
Bizarre their chemistry, their florid junctions,
Under our straightened gaze their rounding eyes.

The Dowry Murder

The danger of biscuit-coloured silk
Is how it just reveals you, the chill
Of the balloon material swaying
In the wind that is not there — the part
Of my body that deals with it needs churching,
Where I keep secret house, a room within
A room, or an organic, touch-dry garden
Where I sit upon my hair. From deep-set
Windows I contemplate the immature moon
Upon the louvered roof of the orangery,
The snow-well thatched with straw, my
Moorish fabrics sapient with
My love of heavy clothing.
Though my railway novel ends
With the bride's sari catching fire
While cooking succotash, something about
The light that is just there musters
A last kiss, your clutch on my familiar stem,
Then your head falling off into a drawer.

Lucina

1 *January*

Today the winter cries, I am the winter,
Not the belted footman ushering the spring:
That's how my body fools itself on the calendar,
Its once-white bean fields monitor
A lip-soft ferning, little shell-pink gardens,
Their wedding-day petals ending in a point:

This is a measure of your place, your plateau,
Where tufted seeds of southernwood are tied
In a muslin bag between the breasts,
Or eaten warm in bread to make them full,
And not the flower that loses perfume, but our senses
Lulled, like babies soothed with dill.

2 *Losing*

Out at the neck of the lough between
The whiskey-coloured clouds, the church
Exposes no more of itself than a house, with
No less grace than water licking the land

In the fattening moon, its muslin veined
And roomy as a canvas, or the seasony
Raspberries, the warm ponds losing what they give,
Creamy with fish as a merry-go-round.

3 *Pica*

We are having a Chinese winter, winds blowing
From Africa bring us the illusion of heavy rain:
And what escorts us is our civilization of pain,
Our rooming-in on Martyrs' Road, or sucking clementines,
As if the house might read how we enjoyed ourselves,
Seeing us through wines . . . . The years torpedoed
My small round world of sugar, with its softened
Wall. Crook-lying in the roof of my mouth, they
Visit me like a graveyard in the evening, full
Of stage-fright, till they break in half
The fastened mind of springtime, areolae
On my milkless bluish breasts.

4 *Lacewood*

I let one lace into the other:
I turn the sapwood of this year
Into the heartwood of the next, and share
The willow's shortest winter, the resilience
Of the ash whose twigs surround you
As you sleep — this is my wind-shaped
Service, my tulip tree a self-sown
Centrepiece in the lawn, and in the house
No hawthorn bush or elder, plants without
Thorns, like flightless birds, stags
Shorn on the velvet farm.

5 *Lamps*

Flowerlike, jailors of light,
They do not let the mind wander
From its sunpath into forest,
From its waistline into ragged muscle,
But pilot into evening as a melody
Alarms the day, dipping dragonflies,
The angled lilies' milky blue,
Flesh tones trapped in the body of the base,
The feverish saucers of seamstresses.

6 *The Sailor*

I am not alone, and not thinking evil:
I'm in a room full of cushions, such a shaky
Nest, I fear you might eliminate,
Abbreviate me, tiring of my mild fingers,
Clear as a telegram, at work below
Your silvery breasts; in this subdued light
I track you like a submarine,
Your night-born murmurings, my craft
As bumpy as a walnut in your squally sea,
My meshy anchor glowing like the cobalt
Head of a god, whose voice transforms
Your stubble into floss, and sends me packing
On a shoe-horn, where your belladonna eyes
Dilate like a dealer's in jade.

7 *The Newborn*

My china animals face into the room:
I have opened all the locks, that you might
Pass safely through a swarm of bees,
Or safely stare into the poppy's centre
Without meeting any lightwaves longer than blue.

The hammock of your eyes, like a woman's
Apron falling off, will find a parting
In my hair, a loaf broken open,
The secretive sky, all its mystic vines and cobwebs,
Sensing feebly the arrival of boats.

8 *The Moon Pond*

I thought this morning of my yellowed Juliette cap,
Its head-dress of artificial pearls that I wore once,
And never wore again . . . . It is not the same
With this bright moon pond where, they say,
If you come once you'll likely come again,
Fed slowly by the natural canal, where the otter swims
You dreamt had made you pregnant.

As with an egg I close my mouth, with an egg
I open it again, my May Day rising, after
My warrior's sleep, and crossing the fat churchyard
Left by a green Christmas, the souls of the dead
As thick as bees in an uncut meadow round me.
I leave a bowl of spring water womanly on the table
For your wild and nameless sprays before they withered.

I leave a stack of salt fallen from a thimble,
A measure of milk with a cock's step of butter,
Coming in hills and going in mountains:
For this milk-fevered lady is the round-eyed child
Listening with bated breath to the singalong
Of birds that, waking in the heart of rain,
Would just as boldly start to mate again.

The Aphrodisiac

She gave it out as if it were
A marriage or a birth, some other
Interesting family event, that she
Had finished sleeping with him, that
Her lover was her friend. It was his heart
She wanted, the bright key to his study,
Not the menacings of love. So he is
Banished to his estates, to live
Like a man in a glasshouse; she has taken to
A little cap of fine white lace
In the mornings, feeds her baby
In a garden you could visit blindfold
For its scent alone:
                          But though a ray of grace
Has fallen, all her books seem as frumpish
As the last year's gambling game, when she
Would dress in pink taffeta, and drive
A blue phaeton, or in blue, and drive
A pink one, with her black hair supported
By a diamond comb, floating about
Without panniers. How his most
Caressing look, his husky whisper suffocates her,
This almost perfect power of knowing
More than a kept woman. The between-maid
Tells me this is not the only secret staircase.
Rumour has it she's taken to rouge again.

The Truth Room

If I were to plant a tree in my handkerchief
Of a garden, it would be a tree of heaven
Which will grow in ash or gravel — like the jewelweed,
Its roots will travel stone, its seeds
Fall fast in a still room. There would be no danger
In our paths thus crossing, it will never come
To resemble me, my cousin of a touch-me-not,
It does not suppress its buds till such
Untimeliness, it takes the cold to break them.

I would want it to bring its moods with it,
Whether it is given to branching low, its branches
Given to wandering. Without trees
I am a moon-walker, I feel breezes
When the whole world is becalmed, in an
Unbreathable sky. From some secret place
Where colour troubles me, I shake a yellow dust.
And yet the very heart of a tree is dead,
Its life is all on the surface, if air reaches it

It leaves the centre hollow and each stage
Of wrapping gone sleepy, as they say of pears,
With rottenness. Still it bends its dead heart
To the light, it is this death that supports it,
Growing harder, as a frozen cloud, dilute
Or buoyant, wills itself to sleep,
Turning inside out, inventing its own sweetness.
It will be to everyone's relief when it starts
Asserting itself, we can't avoid the feeling

It is only really there if it's covered with flowers,
Though frivolity comes easy only to the almond
In a countryside not prone to femininities:
And their prettiness depends on such deceitful
Summers, they leave their ends ajar like naked

Eggs or fecund eyes, while the tree keeps resting
All its nervy, hapless leaves. Its foliage
Always looks as if it has been slept in;
One couldn't call that brown a festive colour:

But unless the purpose of fruit is just
To distance itself, or be crushed, one must wait
Four seasons to see a place, how leaf-fall sums it up.
Then I would call my house 'Falling Water',
Like a truth room where my symptoms feel at home;
And the city's early spring might make a freedom
I thought I had averted stir within me,
With its streets of seeding cloud, its sky's
Plump countrifiedness, blue as God intended.

Next Day Hill

Who knows, you might receive in time for Christmas
A book with primrose edges and a mirror
In the cover. Like a room decorated
At different periods, you will feel it
Like a draught, a shaft of white coming
Long-postponed out of a blue room,
The thin, straight stalk of a woman. It is when
One tries to recount a dream, going on,
Going on, the shyness of other people
Stops mattering, you put it in a cage

Until your lips are quite rested. Is this
Treating a friendship like glass, this great
Temptation to unfold the labour
One had to go through to get back
To the proper size? I wanted so much
To get down again to a place full of old
Summers, Mexican hats, soft fruitwood
Furniture, and less moon, the porch-light
And the leaves catching one another's glance,
Firm clouds not pulled out of shape by wind.

But I am writing here in the dark
Purple sitting-room, the buttons scarcely meeting
On my pink shirt with the pearl collar,
The baby near the stove feeding
Strawberries to our ancient tortoise,
As if neither could go to the other:
Upstairs, the hard beds, the dimity
Curtains, the dreadful Viking strain
Of the study's brick floor where
My poems thicken in the desk.

I am waiting like a sundowner
For the gift of all travel, the first
Steering star, or a man turned down
Forever by the only girl. Call her
Elizabeth, he soaks himself in the comfort
Of her name till a kind of mist
Covers the sky that's all exposed,
A gallant white, inside and out,
And gathers its spine to wedge itself
Somewhere tight, beyond the reach of the mirror.

The Flitting

'You wouldn't believe all this house has cost me —
In body-language terms, it has turned me upside down.'
I've been carried from one structure to the other
On a chair of human arms, and liked the feel
Of being weightless, that fraternity of clothes . . . .
Now my own life hits me in the throat, the bumps
And cuts of the walls as telling
As the poreholes in strawberries, tomato seeds.
I cover them for safety with these Dutch girls
Making lace, or leaning their almond faces
On their fingers with a mandolin, a dreamy
Chapelled ease abreast this other turquoise-turbanned,
Glancing over her shoulder with parted mouth.

She seems a garden escape in her unconscious
Solidarity with darkness, clove-scented
As an orchid taking fifteen years to bloom,
And turning clockwise as the honeysuckle.
Who knows what importance
She attaches to the hours?
Her narrative secretes its own values, as mine might
If I painted the half of me that welcomes death
In a faggotted dress, in a peacock chair,
No falser biography than our casual talk
Of losing a virginity, or taking a life, and
No less poignant if dying
Should consist in more than waiting.

I postpone my immortality for my children,
Little rock-roses, cushioned
In long-flowering sea-thrift and metrics,
Lacking elemental memories:

I am well-earthed here as the digital clock,
Its numbers flicking into place like overgrown farthings
On a bank where once a train
Ploughed like an emperor living out a myth
Through the cambered flesh of clover and wild carrot.

Power-Cut

The moon is salmon as a postage-stamp
Over the tonsured trees, a rise-and-fall lamp
In a cracked ice ceiling. The cruelty
Of road conditions flushes summer near,
As the storm seal hangs along the pier.

My dishes on the draining-board
Lie at an even keel, the baby lowered
Into his lobster-pot pen; my sponge
Disintegrates in water like a bird's nest,
A permanent wave gone west.

These plotted holes of days my keep-net shades,
Soluble as refuse in canals; the old flame
Of the candle sweats in the night, its hump
A dowager's with bones running thin:
The door-butler lets the rain begin.

The Heiress

You say I should stay out of the low
Fields; though my hands love dark,
I should creep till they are heart-shaped,
Like Italian rooms no longer hurt by sun.

When I look at the striped marble of the glen,
I see the husbandry of a good spadesman,
Lifting without injury, or making sure
Where the furrow is this year the ridge
Will be the next; and my pinched grain,
Hanging like a window on the smooth spot
Of a mountain, or a place for fawns, watches
Your way with horses, your delicate Adam work.

But I am lighter of a son, through my slashed
Sleeves the inner sleeves of purple keep remembering
The moment exactly, remembering the birth
Of an heiress means the gobbling of land.

Dead leaves do not necessarily
Fall; it is not coldness, but the tree itself
That bids them go, preventing their destruction.
So I walk along the beach, unruly, I drop
Among my shrubbery of seaweed my black acorn buttons.

The Mast Year

Some kinds of trees are ever eager
To populate new ground, the oak or pine.
Though beech can thrive on many soils
And carve itself an empire, its vocation
Is gentler; it casts a shade for wildflowers
Adapted to the gloom, which feed
Like fungus on its rot of bedstraw leaves.

It makes an awkward neighbour, as does
The birch, that lashes out in gales, and fosters
Intimacy with toadstools, till they sleep
In the benevolence of each other's smells,
Never occupying many sites for long:
The thin red roots of alder vein
The crumbled bank, the otter's ruptured door.

Bee-keepers love the windbreak sycamore,
The twill of hanging flowers that the beech
Denies the yew — its waking life so long
It lets the stylish beechwood
Have its day, as winded oaks
Lay store upon their Lammas growth,
The thickening of their dreams.